THE BLACK SINISTER

THE BLACK SINISTER™

DEATH RIDES A BULLET

THE BLACK SINISTER
created by TROY NIXEY & KAARE ANDREWS

Written by KAARE ANDREWS
Drawn by TROY NIXEY
Colored by DAVE McCAIG
Lettered by PAT BROSSEAU

Cover art by TROY NIXEY with DAVE McCAIG

Dark Horse Books

President & Publisher **Mike Richardson**

Editors **Daniel Chabon and Brendan Wright**

Assistant Editor **Cardner Clark** Designer **Patrick Satterfield**

Logo Designer **Charles Brock** Digital Art Technician **Melissa Martin**

THE BLACK SINISTER

This volume collects chapters 1–6 of the story "The Black Sinister: Death Rides a Bullet," originally published in *Dark Horse Presents* #26–#31.

Library of Congress Cataloging-in-Publication Data

Names: Andrews, Kaare, author, creator. | Nixey, Troy, artist, creator. | McCaig, Dave, colourist, artist. | Brosseau, Pat, letterer.
Title: The Black Sinister : death rides a bullet / written by Kaare Andrews ; drawn by Troy Nixey ; colored by Dave McCaig ; lettered by Pat Brosseau ; cover art by Troy Nixey with Dave McCaig.
Description: First edition. | Milwaukie, OR : Dark Horse Books, 2017. | "The Black Sinister created by Troy Nixey & Kaare Andrews" | "This volume collects chapters 1-6 of the story "The Black Sinister: Death Rides a Bullet," originally published in Dark Horse Presents #26-#31."
Identifiers: LCCN 2017003667 | ISBN 9781506703374 (hardback)
Subjects: LCSH: Comic books, strips, etc. | BISAC: COMICS & GRAPHIC NOVELS / Horror. | COMICS & GRAPHIC NOVELS / Superheroes. | COMICS & GRAPHIC NOVELS / Literary.
Classification: LCC PN6728.B51937 A53 2017 | DDC 741.5/973–dc23
LC record available at https://lccn.loc.gov/2017003667

Published by
Dark Horse Books
A division of Dark Horse Comics, Inc.
10956 SE Main Street • Milwaukie, OR 97222

DarkHorse.com

To find a comics shop in your area, call the Comic Shop Locator Service toll-free at 1-888-266-4226.
International Licensing: (503) 905-2377

First edition: July 2017
ISBN 978-1-50670-337-4

1 3 5 7 9 10 8 6 4 2
Printed in China

chapter one

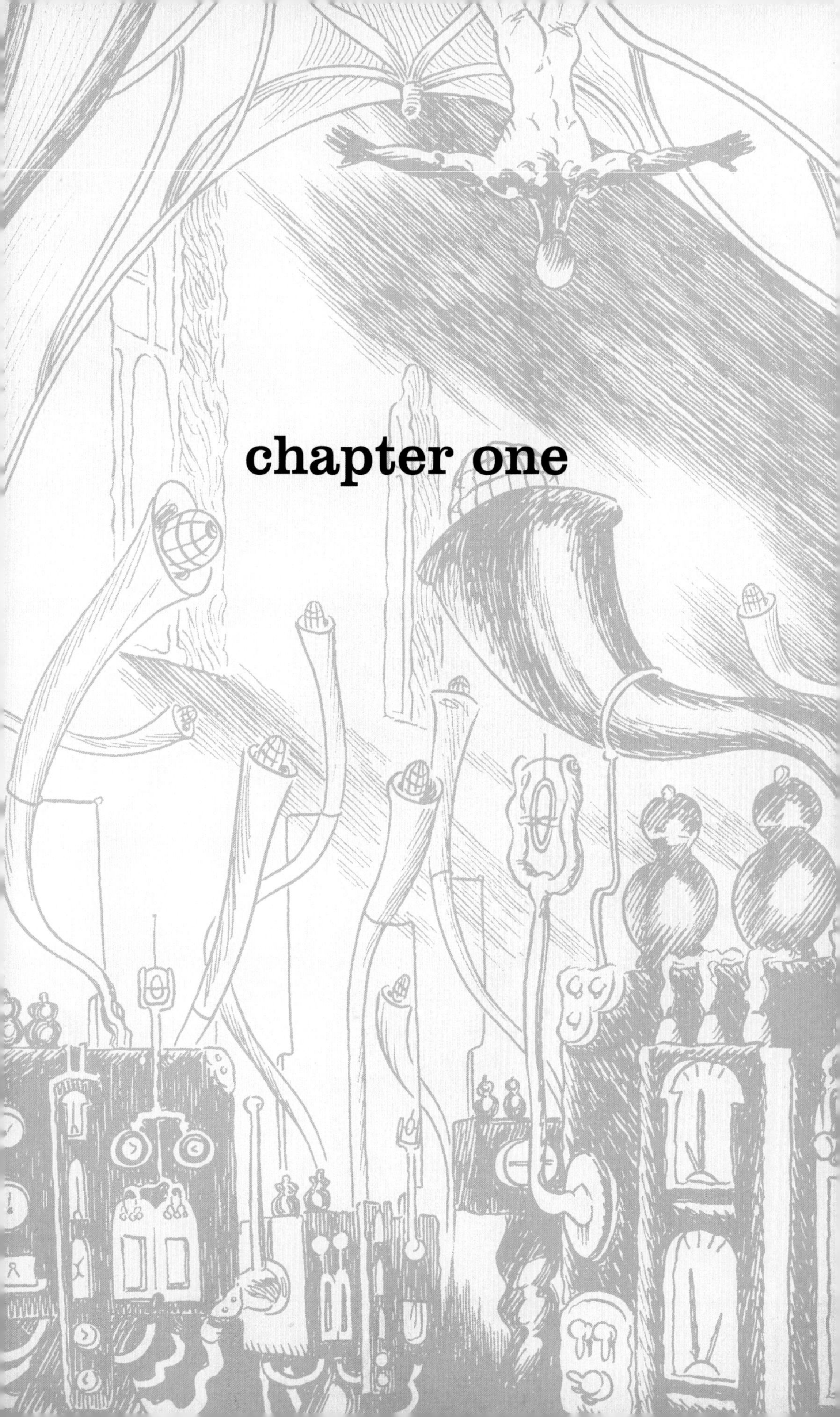

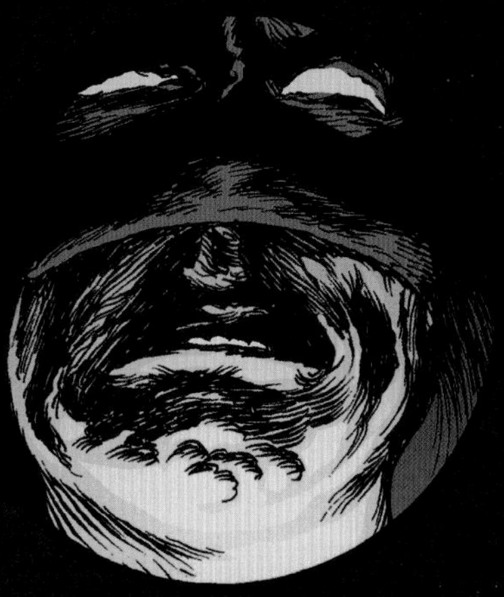

The lie that the button pushers tell themselves. That they can become more.
That any man could climb the mountain, steal fire from the gods, and return a hero.
And so they push the buttons HARDER, FASTER...
But real heroes aren't created--they're born. Wealth. Privilege. Power.
The true Hero's Journey isn't to rise above the button pushers--but to accept that you've been above them all along.
LEON
BRING EMERSON BLACK TO JUSTICE!
HE CRIPPLED MY MOTHER FOR PARKING IN A HANDICAPPED SPOT!
EMERSON BLACK IS INSANE!
CUT OFF ALL MY TOES FOR JAYWALKING!
HEY HEY, HO HO. EMERSON BLACK HAS GOT TO GO!
RENT
W.F.S.
HIGH !!!!!!
LACK BE ONE
NO
NOT A HERO
EXTRA! EXTRA! BLACK CLEARED OF CHARGES!
TAXES RISE AS COAL CITY ORDERED TO REPAY BLACK'S LEGAL FEES!
CITIZENS ORDERED TO SIGN CLASS-ACTION APOLOGY!
CROWDS READY TO RIOT!
EXTRA! EXTRA! PAPERBOY DELIVERS NEWS TO CITY HALL!

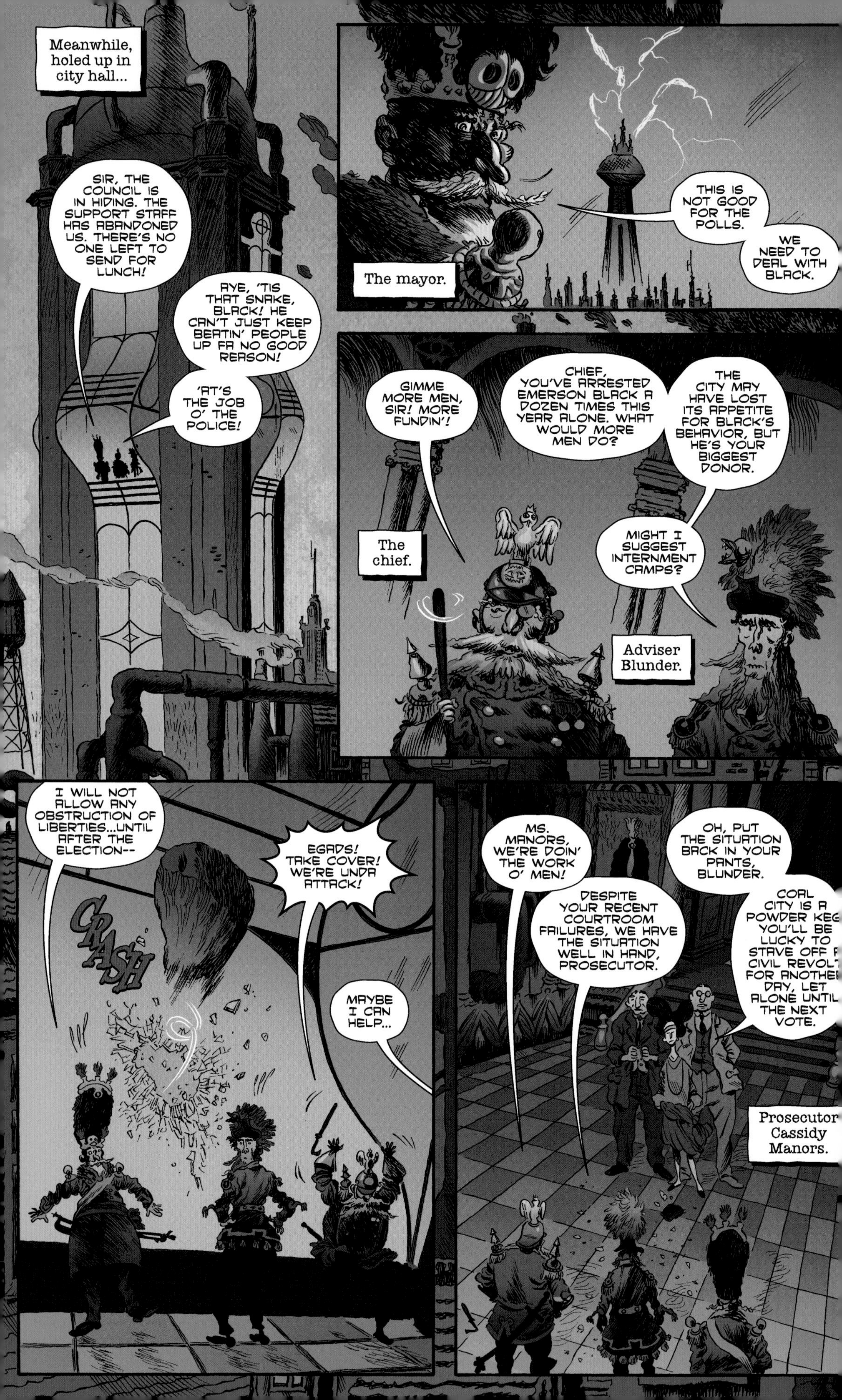
Meanwhile, holed up in city hall...
SIR, THE COUNCIL IS IN HIDING. THE SUPPORT STAFF HAS ABANDONED US. THERE'S NO ONE LEFT TO SEND FOR LUNCH!
AYE, 'TIS THAT SNAKE, BLACK! HE CAN'T JUST KEEP BEATIN' PEOPLE UP FA NO GOOD REASON!
'AT'S THE JOB O' THE POLICE!
The mayor.
THIS IS NOT GOOD FOR THE POLLS.
WE NEED TO DEAL WITH BLACK.
The chief.
GIMME MORE MEN, SIR! MORE FUNDIN'!
CHIEF, YOU'VE ARRESTED EMERSON BLACK A DOZEN TIMES THIS YEAR ALONE. WHAT WOULD MORE MEN DO?
THE CITY MAY HAVE LOST ITS APPETITE FOR BLACK'S BEHAVIOR, BUT HE'S YOUR BIGGEST DONOR.
MIGHT I SUGGEST INTERNMENT CAMPS?
Adviser Blunder.
I WILL NOT ALLOW ANY OBSTRUCTION OF LIBERTIES...UNTIL AFTER THE ELECTION--
CRASH
EGADS! TAKE COVER! WE'RE UNDA ATTACK!
MAYBE I CAN HELP...
MS. MANORS, WE'RE DOIN' THE WORK O' MEN!
DESPITE YOUR RECENT COURTROOM FAILURES, WE HAVE THE SITUATION WELL IN HAND, PROSECUTOR.
OH, PUT THE SITUATION BACK IN YOUR PANTS, BLUNDER.
COAL CITY IS A POWDER KEG. YOU'LL BE LUCKY TO STAVE OFF A CIVIL REVOLT FOR ANOTHER DAY, LET ALONE UNTIL THE NEXT VOTE.
Prosecutor Cassidy Manors.

WITH RESPECT, MR. MAYOR, YOU'RE COMPLETELY F--
FATHER built Coal City in his own image. A beast of brickwork cancer.
BLACK HYDRO bathes in soot and coughs up charcoal lungs.
While BLACK MANOR rises about the stench.
YOUR SOYMILK AND GLUTEN-FREE COOKIES, SIR.
HAVE YOU SEEN THE CROWDS GATHERING OUTSIDE?
PERHAPS THE RABBLE COULD USE A LITTLE OF THE OLD POINT AND SHOOT?
DO YOU BLAME THE SHEEP FOR WHERE THE SHEPHERD HAS LED THEM?
I WILL DEAL WITH THE MAYOR IN GOOD TIME, DANBY. THE WAY MY FATHER DEALT WITH THOSE WHO STOOD IN HIS WAY.
IF YOU'RE LOOKING FOR TARGET PRACTICE, START OUTSIDE.
BUT, DANBY?... NO HEAD-SHOTS... NO VITAL ORGANS.
Danby.
OH. *SIGH* ALL RIGHT, SIR...
Family time is precious to me. A chance to reconnect with those I love.
And I love HER so...
MOTHER, I NEED TO KNOW...

Every night I stand before her and ask forgiveness.
BLAM
PLEASE, NO!
BLAM
JUST DELIVERING THE MILK-- AGH!!
...DO I DISAPPOINT YOU?
BLAM
AAGGH!
BLAM
MY LEGS! I CAN'T FEEL MY...
My guilt, I see in his eyes.
FATHER, EACH MORNING YOU CHAIN ME TO THESE ROCKS. WATCH THE VULTURES TEAR OPEN MY INNARDS.
MUNCH! MUNCH!
My pain...
MOTHER, EACH NIGHT YOU PUSH THE GUTS INSIDE AND SEW ME BACK UP.
...tastes like her.
I ALLOW THE CHAINS SO I MAY STILL FEEL YOUR HANDS MOTHER.
They say that without family, a man trembles in the cold.
And so I hold myself next to the fire.
And let it burn.
OF COURSE. MOTHER WAS JUST TUCKING ME IN.
THAT'S BETTER. MAY I SUGGEST AN EARLY NIGHT, SIR?

Back in the
ayor's office...
Poke.
ALLOW ME TO INTRODUCE YOU TO THE BETTER BUSINESS AMBASSADORS.
Choke.
YA BROUGHT THE MOB TA CITY HALL?!
Big Red.
MR. MAYOR, THERE'S A NATURAL BALANCE TO THINGS.
THERE'S BREAKIN' THE LAW AND ENFORCING IT. IT'S THE PISTONS WHAT MAKE THE WORLD GO ROUND.
THESE ARE STRANGE TIMES, INDEED, AND YOU'RE NOT THE ONLY PARTY RECONSIDERING HIS IDEOLOGY.
THE BBA HAS GONE LEGIT.
HORSE-RADISH! WHAT IS IT YER AFTER, YA LITTLE PUKE?!
GIT BACK ON YER HORSE AND SELL YER MAGIC BEANS ELSEWHERE, YA CHARLATAN!
CHIEF, A LITTLE RESPECT. WE ARE SIMPLY HERE TO OFFER OUR HELP.
AND JUST HOW DO YOU INTEND TO HELP US DEAL WITH AN ARMED MULTIBILLIONAIRE SOCIOPATH?
I'M UP AGAINST IT, BLUNDER. LET'S HEAR THEM OUT.
WHAT'S YOUR ANGLE, RED?
OH, ME HEAD...
PERHAPS YOU'VE HEARD OF...THE MANIAK DEVICE?
WHAT?!
MANIAK

THE--THE SAME DEVICE WE DROPPED ON THE KRUCKS TO END THE WAR? HOW DID YOU--
ARE YA MAD?! WE'RE TRYING TO SAVE THE CITY, NO' LEVEL IT!
THE BBA IS HANDING US A REAL OPPORTUNITY, MR. MAYOR.
EVEN IF YOU ACTUALLY HAD THIS DEVICE, I COULD NEVER UNLEASH IT ON MY OWN CITIZENS...
BETTER TO BE A MAYOR OF A SMALL CLEANUP SITE THAN NOT A MAYOR AT ALL...
THIS IS JUST MADNESS-- OOF!
KRACK
HAVE NO FEAR... 'TIS ONLY PETE... ME INFORMANT...
Newsboy Pete.
CHIEF, DIDJA GET MY NOTE?!
YEAH... THANKS, LADDIE...
SOME NUT'S HOLED UP WITH A KID AT GUNPOINT! HE'S DEMANDIN' TO SPEAK TO THE MAYOR!
HOLY POTATOES! SCRAMBLE THE SQUAD! WE'VE GOT TA TAKE CARE OF THIS BEFORE BLACK CATCHES WIND!
THIS IS NOT GOOD FOR THE POLLS.
THINGS WERE SIMPLER ON THE PLAYGROUND. REMEMBER THOSE DAYS, BEN?
CAME DOWN TO IT, YOU COULD SETTLE THINGS WITH YOUR FISTS.

WE'LL GIVE YA WHATEVER YA WANT, JUST HURRY UP!
I AIN'T COMIN' DOWN TILL I TALK TO THE MAYOR!
CUT TH' LADDIE LOOSE, AND WE'LL HAVE A NICE CHAT ABOUT IT.
WE DON' HAVE MUCH TIME BEFORE YOU-KNOW-WHO INVITES HIMSELF TO DA PARTY.
LANCE
SANDWICH
GOLD
Meanwhile, in the secret monitoring room deep underneath Black Manor...
ZZZZZ
TODAY'S STOCK MARKET TUMBLED AS BLACK INDUSTRIES FORCED THE CLOSURE OF ITS LAST MAJOR COMPETITOR...
THE INQUIRY INTO ILLEGAL WIRETAPPING FROM BLACK NEWS CAME TO A CLOSE TODAY AS ANOTHER WITNESS VANISHED...
SCRAMBLE ALL CARS! SCRAMBLE ALL CARS!
THE KIDNAPPER'S ASKING FOR THE MAYOR!
YOU GET ME THE MAYOR, OR WHO KNOWS WHAT I MIGHT DO!
DON'T BE A FOOL, MAN!
OH, WHAT'S THIS, THEN?
SHALL I READY THE OLD GIRL FOR YOU, SIR?
HE'LL COME FOR US ALL!

All around me is his name.
He taunts me. Powerful. Intimidating.
If there was no one left to hold him at bay...
The fools. They don't know the danger.
When Father finally keeled over in a puddle of tar, I inherited the burden of defending Coal City...
Even from itself.
WOOOOOOM
LOOK UP! INTO THE NIGHT...!
INTO THE DARK!
INTO THE PITCH... BLACK...!
To show man light, first show him night.
Else there is only gray.
?
I'll judge their souls as black as coal.
And rip the soot away...
BLACK ATTACK!
HE'S COMING!
QUICK, HIDE YOUR SIGNS!
STAY STRONG, TIMMY.
I DON'T THINK THIS I GOING TO END WELL, FATHER.
FOR ANYON
KEEP THE DAY, I'LL SAVE THE NIGHT!
AND MAKE THINGS RIGHT, DESPITE THE FRIGHT.
THE SINISTER TAKES FLIGHT!

chapter two

We're all special. We are all unique. Precious little snowflakes.
That is what your parents told you. But hold those flakes against the fire and see how they stand up.
The "individual" is simply a fractal.
Each uniqueness simply a subset of a larger pattern.
YOU GET ME THE MAYOR, YA HEAR?! OR THIS RANDOM LITTLE BOY I'VE TAKEN HOLD OF GETS IT!
BECAUSE OF REASONS!
ROOMS
ROOMS
You are not unique. You are not special.
I'M PLEADIN' WIT' YOU, MAN! GIVE UP BEFA' IT'S TOO LATE! LET THE LADDIE GO!
You will not be treated any different than the other fragile crystals of water.
I'M NOT DOIN' NOTHING TILL I'VE TALKED TO THE MAYOR!
I AIN'T SCARED A NO COPPERS!
You will fall. You will melt.
And then you will ascend back to your pointless beginnings in the sky. Ready to start the meaningless trip again.
While I keep the fires BURNING below.
YA DAMNED FOOL...

Meanwhile, watching from the tower windows of city hall...
MR. MAYOR, SIR. THIS IS TERRIBLE--TERRIBLE. I'M PECKISH AND HYPOGLYCEMIC. AND NOW THIS HORRIBLE DRAFT...
MR. MAYOR, THE BETTER BUSINESS AMBASSADORS SIMPLY WANT TO HELP.
THE MANIAK DEVICE HAS THE ABILITY TO WIPE OUT THREE CITY BLOCKS. JUST THINK OF ALL THE REVENUE OPPORTUNITIES FROM NEW PARKING STRUCTURES.
MR. MAYOR, THIS IS YOUR CITY, YOUR BILLIONAIRE SUPERHERO SOCIOPATH. YOUR PROBLEM.
BUT IT DOESN'T HAVE TO BE.
BEN, HE MAKES SENSE. SHIFT SOME OF THE WORKLOAD ONTO RED.
YOU HAVE SUCH A VERY... HARD...JOB. MAKE SOME ROOM IN YOUR LIFE FOR THE MORE PLEASURABLE THINGS...
PROSECUTOR MANORS CAN BE VERY PERSUASIVE, MR. MAYOR.
LET HER.
I'M NO IDIOT! I HAVE MY OWN PLANS! I'VE BEEN PREPARING FOR THIS DAY!
EMERSON BLACK HAS PUSHED ME TOO FAR. BLUNDER, FIND ME THE TELERADIO!
OOF!

My targets are elow me. ALL OF HEM. But at the noment I'm only nterested in the ne.
OPERATION NIGHT LIGHT. OPERATION NIGHT LIGHT...DO YOU COPY?
YUM-YUM TATI TOMATOES
he cowards. ave they rgotten who ontrols Black eleradio?
BONJOUR, MONSIEUR MAYOR!
NO, NO NAMES, DAMMIT!
PARDON MY FRENCH..."BEEG POPPA."
OUI, OUI! YOU GOT EET, MONSIEUR MAYOR!
THUNDERBIKES, THE TIME HAS COME. ARE YOU READY?
WHY DO I EVEN...
YOU HEARD ZEE MAN. HELMET UP AND MOUNT ZEE BEASTS!
Traitors. Rats. Do they think they can scurry through the shadows of the night, undetected?
I am the shadows...
THUNDERBIKES, ***EN ROUTE!***
I am the night...

I am the BLACK... and the SINISTER!
ACTEEVATE!
FLYEEENG ROCKITZ!!...
I AM THE GRIM, DARK HORROR OF...
OHHHH, THIS LOOKS LIKE FUN...
PREEPARE FOR ZEE ASSS-SAULT!
ASSS-SAULT!

MY WORD...
MY EYEEYYEEZ! I AM ABLAZE!
LE ARRARRGH!!
EEK!
I'M ABOUT TO SICK UP.
That was certainly refreshing. Always enjoy a little evening stroll.
AND NOW BACK TO THE MATTER AT HAND.
THIS IS YER LAST CHANCE, PALLIE! YER OUT O' TIME!
GIVE YERSELF UP!
NO, DON'T GIVE UP!
TIMMY, WE GOTTA STAY STRONG-- FOR EACH OTHER. DO WHATEVER IT TAKES TO STAY TOGETHER!
FATHER? I'M SCARED.

YOU DARE TAKE HOSTAGE AN INNOCENT CHILD!
CHILDREN ARE THE UNTAPPED WORK FORCE OF THE FUTURE!
HE'S BLUFFING. HE WOULDN'T...
THE MAYOR WILL HELP US! IF I CAN JUST TALK TO HIM...HE'S A FAMILY MAN. HE'LL UNDERSTAND!
AND CHEAP LABOR MUST BE PROTECTED AT ALL COSTS!
BOO.

NO, PLEASE...
FIEND, LOOK INTO MY PITCH-DARK HEART...
NO...
TELL ME WHAT YOU SEE...
NOOO! TIMMY!! NO!!
YOU KILLED MY SON!
YOUR... OH. CRAP.
OOPS?

chapter three

SWEET LORD, BLACK. WHAT HAVE YA DONE?
I JUST WANTED TO TALK TO THE MAYOR ABOUT THE CUSTODY RULING.
HIS MOTHER HAD PROBLEMS.
BUT NO ONE LISTENED.
AND SO I DID THIS ONE DESPERATE, CRAZY THING...
AND YOU KILLED HIM FOR IT.
EASY, BUTTON PUSHER. THIS ISN'T MY FAULT...
KILLED HIM FOR THE LOVE OF HIS FATHER.
EMERSON BLACK, YOU ARE A SCOURGE AND A FIEND!
DAMN US BOTH TO HELL!
W-WAIT-- WAIT! FOR THE LOVE OF PROFITS!

SPLAT
AND NOW HE'S KILLED THE FATHER TOO...
YOU SAW! YOU ALL SAW... GASP...HE PUSHED ME! ME!
YOUR BENEFACTOR, YOUR PROTECTOR... YOUR F-FRIEND?...
HOW MANY MORE OF US ARE YOU GONNA THROW OFF A ROOFTOP?
CHILD KILLER...
COWARD...
WELL NOW, LOOKS LIKE LUNCH...
CHIEF?...GASP... THIS MOB OF IDIOTS IS THREATENING TO RIOT...A DANGER TO PUBLIC...SAFETY...
LADS?

CHIEF!!!
'TIS A BEAUTIFUL DAY...
OH MY...
THEY'RE TEARING HIM APART!
AND THAT'S HOW YOU WIN AN ELECTION. CONGRATULATIONS, SIR! NOW SHALL WE ORDER TAKE-OUT?
I APOLOGIZE FOR THE INTRUSION, MAYOR. YOU OBVIOUSLY HAVE EVERYTHING UNDER COMPLETE CONTROL.
UM, YES. QUITE!
I'LL SEE MYSELF OUT. SORRY TO BE OF ANY...
TROUBLE? SIR?
THERE... OOF!... DAMN WELL BETTER BE!
I'LL BE RIGHT UP--

FOOOSH
SIR, I DO ENJOY THE WAY A KNEECAP OPENS AGAINST THE GENTLE CARESS OF HOT LEAD.
YOU BRING THE KIT?
AAA-OI-OIGH!
BLAM
BLAM BLAM
AAAHHGH
OF COURSE.
A SECOND TRANSPORT IS ON THE WAY, STOCKED TO THE CEILING IN BODY BAGS...
FOR YOUR *REVENGE.*
THEY WILL FIND THEIR WAY BACK TO THE PENS.
I HAVE A DATE WITH THE SHEPHERD.
MAYOR! MAYOR? CAN YE HEAR ME?
ERRIGHGH!
CHIEF! WHAT IS IT? SOUNDS LIKE WORLD WAR FOUR DOWN THERE!

WORSE! BLACK IS BACK!
CAN YOU PUT HIM ON THE TELERADIO? MAYBE I SHOULD SPEAK WITH HIM.
YA WILL INDEED! 'CAUSE THAT CRAZY LOON IS GUNNIN' STRAIGHT FA' CITY HALL!
THE MAYOR HAS LED HIS FLOCK ASTRAY!
AND IN TURN THEY HAVE LED ME TO HIM!

HE WILL BE PUNISHED FOR IT!
CHIEF?
AND HE WILL BURN!
CHIEF?
HOLD IT TOGETHER, MAYOR. LET'S NOT JUMP TO CONCLUSIONS.
WE'RE ALL GOING TO DIE!
BLUNDER, GET RED BACK IN HERE...NOW.
BOOM BOOM BOOM BOOM
When I was a child, I feared my father's hand.
What it could do to me.
Let them feel it.
Let them feel the DARK FLESH.

WE HAD AN AGREEMENT, MAYOR!
BUT YOU TURNED BUTTON PUSHERS INTO SIGN MAKERS!
POLICE INTO HOOLIGANS! OLD LADIES INTO NEW OFFENDERS!
YOU LOST CONTROL... AND NOW I'M TAKING IT BACK!
MAYOR, WE SAID OUR GOODBYES.
PLEASE, RED. THE MAYOR'S READY TO LISTEN NOW.
I'D BE MORE THAN HAPPY TO REOPEN THE DISCUSSIONS...
BUT THE PRICE JUST WENT UP.
THERE'S TWO WAYS THIS CAN GO, MAYOR!
COME OUT IN ONE PIECE...OR ALL OF THEM!
WHAT DO YOU WANT?
POWER. BLACK POWER, TO BE SPECIFIC. BUT I AIN'T LOOKING FOR NO PERCENTAGE. I WANT A PINK SLIP.
HE WOULD NEVER ALLOW IT.
THEN WE CAN SOLVE TWO PROBLEMS. YOURS AND MINE. THE MANIAK HAS BEEN AIRBORNE FOR THIRTY MINUTES. MAYOR, JUST SAY THE WORD.
BLACK THINKS HE CAN INTIMIDATE ME? I'M AN ELECTED GOVERNING OFFICIAL!
THIS CITY CHOSE ME, NOT HIM!
RED, IF YOU CAN PROTECT THE GOOD PEOPLE OF COAL CITY, THE BBA CAN HAVE BLACK POWER. ALL OF IT!
I'LL NEED THAT IN WRITING.

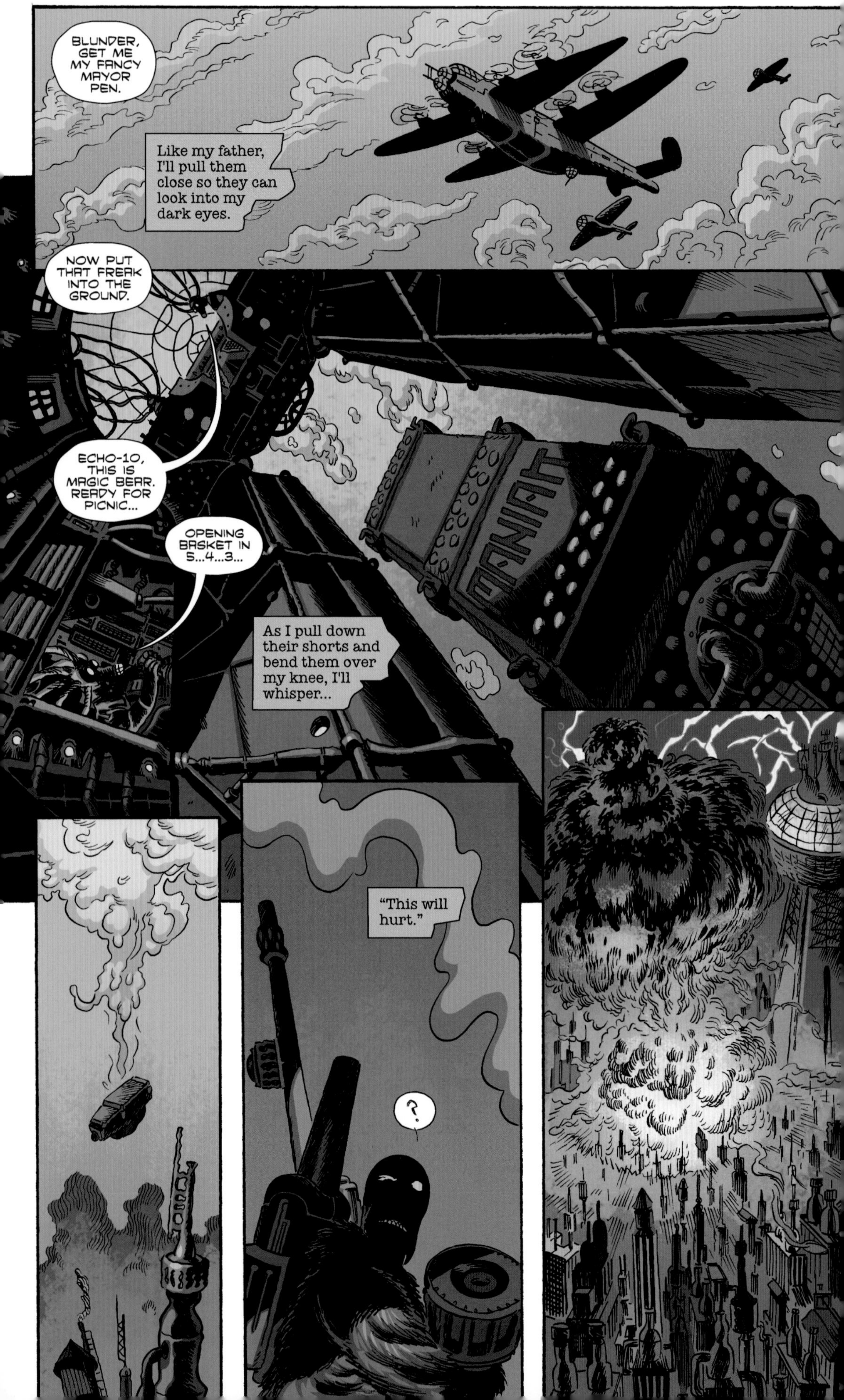
BLUNDER, GET ME MY FANCY MAYOR PEN.
Like my father, I'll pull them close so they can look into my dark eyes.
NOW PUT THAT FREAK INTO THE GROUND.
ECHO-10, THIS IS MAGIC BEAR. READY FOR PICNIC...
OPENING BASKET IN 5...4...3...
As I pull down their shorts and bend them over my knee, I'll whisper...
"This will hurt."
?

chapter four

Hair burned to ash, clothes covered in soot. Their wooden signs smoking cinder...
The thing they always hoped for has happened in front of their eyes.
And all they feel is TERROR.
PING

PING
PING
WWWWHHHRRRR
Money...
Is POWER.
MY FATHER TAUGHT ME, ENOUGH OF IT, AND YOU COULD BUY YOUR WAY OUT OF ANYTHING. EVEN DEATH.
A MANIAK DEVICE, EH? THOSE CRAZY FOOLS.
HE AIN'T DOWN YET, RED.
GIVE HIM TIME, MAYOR. THE MANIAK DEVICE IS UNSTOPPABLE.
SO TELL ME, TIN MAN.
WHAT ARE YOU WORTH?

ESSEX ST

SLAM
WHUP
OOOF
AAAAA
POW
BOO
STAB
BLAM
ZA
BOK
GORE
PUKE
KRA
OFF
WHAM

SECOND-CLASS... REFURBISHED TOASTER...
THAT ALL YOU... GOT?
BOOOM

IT'S FINALLY DONE. HE DID IT. ***WE DID IT!***
EMERSON BLACK IS SENT TO HELL!
CHOKE ON ***THAT,*** BLACK!
SPLLT
STAGE ONE, COMPLETE. STAGE TWO, INITIATE.
THE BEAST ISN'T DONE YET!
CAN'T YOU SEE? HE'S HUNGRY FOR ***MORE--***
SPLLT
RED, YOUR DAMNED BOMB IS TURNING ON THE CROWD! SHUT IT DOWN!
BOOM
I PROMISED TO RUB OUT EMERSON BLACK BY UNLEASHING AN UNSTOPPABLE KILLING MACHINE.
NEVER SAID NOTHIN' ABOUT TURNING IT BACK OFF AGAIN!

FFSSSSSTTT
RUN FA YOUR LIVES! THAT T'ING WILL KILL US ALL!
FFFRRRSSSTTT
WHAT IN THE DIRT AND SPUDS?
CLEAR THE ROAD, YA LOSERS!
BONK
WE DID IT, BOYS! TOOK THE CITY FROM RIGHT UNDER THEIR NOSES!
WHATEVER'S LEFT OF IT, ANYWAYS!
SMASH
HEY! GONNA SCRATCH THE PAINT!

Black.
Fire.
EMERSON?
Death.
IS THAT YOU, MOTHER? HAVE YOU COME TO TUCK ME IN?
Murder.
The boy from the window. He's come for me.
I'M AFRAID NOT, MR. BLACK.
He pulls me to my feet and my arm goes with him.
I wonder how I'm ever going to tie my shoes.
THIS IS NO TIME TO SLEEP. NOT HERE. HE WON'T LET YOU.

chapter five

The streets of Coal City BURN and the buildings smolder in RUINS.
The smoking behemoth stands like some sort of manifestation of death.
But the Maniak is still. Horrifying.
MS. MANORS, HAS THE DESTRUCTION FINALLY PASSED?
BLOOD SUGAR... INCREDIBLY LOW... FEELING FAINT... PECKISH...
IT'S OVER, MAYOR. EMERSON BLACK HAS BEEN DE--
--STROYYYYED!!!!
OH, FOR THE LOVE OF POLLS!
BAM

Meanwhile, in the land of the dead.
THIS PLACE SMELLS... FAMILIAR, KID. LIKE BURNED TOAST AND TOBACCO. ANY IDEA WHERE WE ARE?
IT'S TIMMY, SIR. AND I THINK YOU ALREADY KNOW.
As a figure emerges from the mist...the smell of toast thickens. Crunches.
EMERSON? IS THAT... YOU?
And dark decades' worth of grief spill out onto Black's quivering cheeks.
M-MOTHER?
As Emerson Black finally realizes where he is. HOME.
MAMA!
SO, THE DISGUSTING LITTLE PRODIGAL HAS FINALLY RETURNED.

RETURNED FOR MORE!
MOTHER, NO!!!
RUN, SIR! RUN!!!
IS THAT THE DEVIL, SIR?
WORSE! MY FATHER!
PATHETIC! JUST LIKE YOUR MOTHER.
HIDE ALL YOU WANT, SON. I HAVE AN ETERNITY TO PUNISH YOU.
I THINK I'LL START WITH THE TOENAILS.
WORK MY WAY UP FROM THERE! BWA-HA-HAA!!
SIR, I'M JUST A POOR LITTLE DEAD BOY. I CAN'T SAVE YOU. YOU'RE THE ADULT, SIR!
SIR?
ONE, TWO... CHARCOAL MY SHOE... ONE, TWO, CHARCOAL MY SHOE... ONE, TWO...

GOT YOU!
GRRAAKK
AAGGHH!!
ONE, TWO... ONE, TWO... ONE, TWO...
I THINK YOU'VE FORGOTTEN HOW TO BE A MAN, SIR. LET ME SHOW YOU...
OPEN YOUR EYES, SIR! UGH!!
SIR! ACK!
ONE, TWO, ONE, TWO, ONE, TWO...
A WEEK LATE, HIDING IN YOUR MOTHER'S WOMB! AFRAID OF THE WORLD! KILLING HER WITH YOUR COWARDICE!
GROW UP, SIR!

ALL I NEEDED WAS ANOTHER FOUR YEARS! I WAS GOING TO RETIRE IN THE SUN! LIVE A GOOD LIFE ON FUNNELED INCOME AND STOLEN PENSION MONEY.
THE AMERICAN DREAM!
OH, SHUT UP ALREADY AND FIND ME A SANDWICH!
OR A SMALL PIECE OF *CHEEEEE-EEEEEEESE!!!*
BLUNDER, NO!
JUST A *CRRUUUUMMMB!*
WHAT ARE YOU DOING??!
TAKE HER! SHE'S THE ONE YOU WANT! ***I RELINQUISH ALL GOVERNING AUTHORITY TO MS. MANORS!***
I'M NOBODY NOW! ***NOT WORTH THE EFFORT!***

ALL THOSE YEARS, EMERSON, AND YOU NEVER BROUGHT A FRIEND HOME FOR DINNER.
EVERY BIRTHDAY PARTY UNATTENDED. EVERY SLEEPOVER, ALONE.
I WANTED AN HEIR. ALL I GOT WAS SHAME.
KNEW I HAD TO TOUGHEN YOU UP, BOY! WHATEVER IT TOOK!
BUT YOU WITHERED AND WATCHED ME HURT THE ONLY PERSON THAT LOVED YOU.
YOU COULD HAVE STOPPED ME!
IT WAS YOUR FAULT.
YOU KILLED HER!
ONE, TWO, ONE, TWO, ONE, TWO, ONE, TWO--
GORE
ONE! TWO!
YOU DON'T MAKE SOMETHING STRONG BY STEPPING ON IT.
YOU DON'T KEEP SOMEONE SAFE BY CAGING THEM.
ZZZTTT
ZZZZTT
ZZZZTT
ZZZZTTT

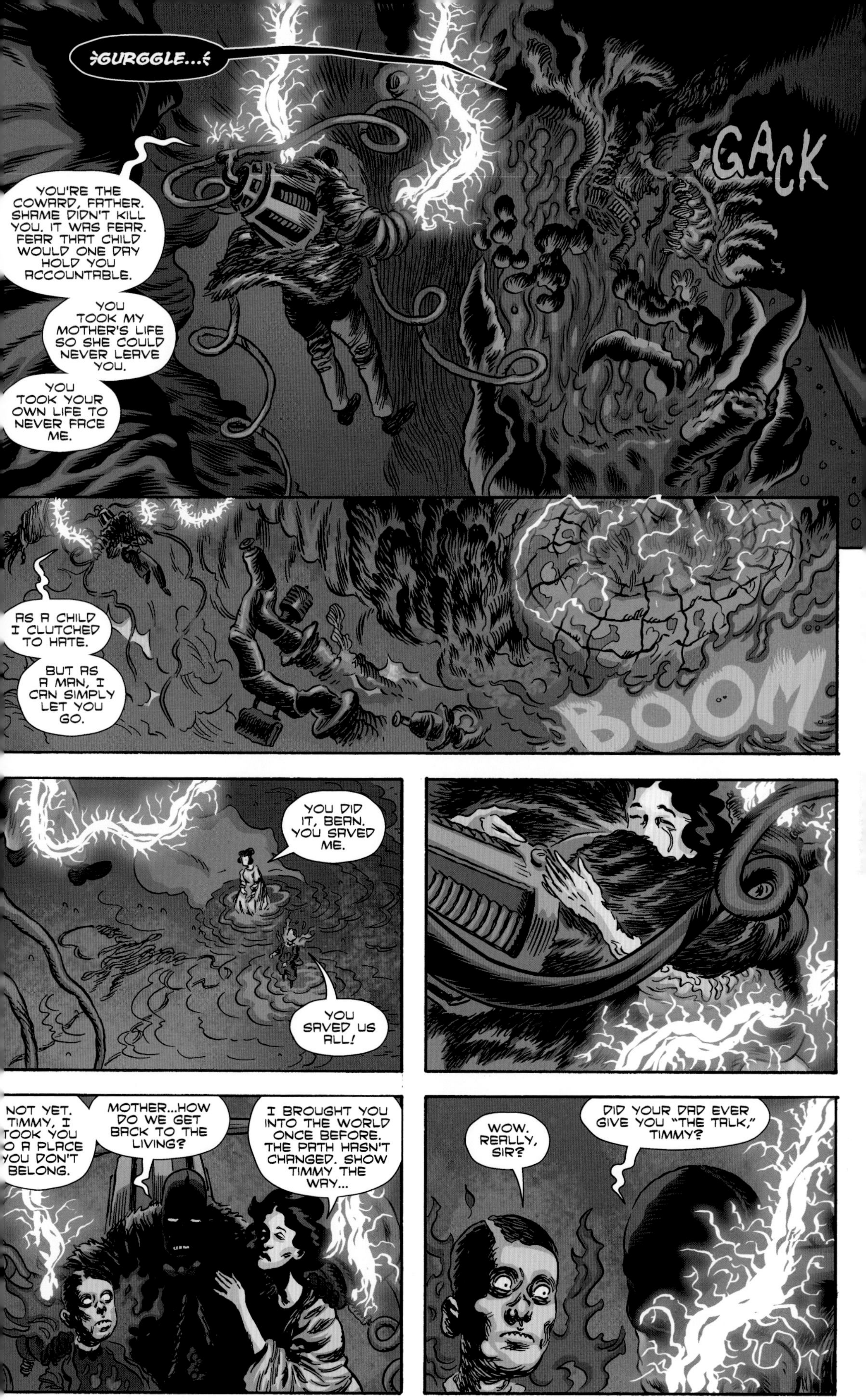
GURGGLE...
GACK
YOU'RE THE COWARD, FATHER. SHAME DIDN'T KILL YOU. IT WAS FEAR. FEAR THAT CHILD WOULD ONE DAY HOLD YOU ACCOUNTABLE.
YOU TOOK MY MOTHER'S LIFE SO SHE COULD NEVER LEAVE YOU.
YOU TOOK YOUR OWN LIFE TO NEVER FACE ME.
AS A CHILD I CLUTCHED TO HATE.
BUT AS A MAN, I CAN SIMPLY LET YOU GO.
BOOM
YOU DID IT, BEAN. YOU SAVED ME.
YOU SAVED US ALL!
NOT YET. TIMMY, I TOOK YOU O A PLACE YOU DON'T BELONG.
MOTHER...HOW DO WE GET BACK TO THE LIVING?
I BROUGHT YOU INTO THE WORLD ONCE BEFORE. THE PATH HASN'T CHANGED. SHOW TIMMY THE WAY...
DID YOUR DAD EVER GIVE YOU "THE TALK," TIMMY?
WOW. REALLY, SIR?

They say everyone experiences the miracle of birth at least once: their own.
34TH ST
That the pain of being forced from the warmth of the womb and into the cold world makes you strong. Makes you ready.
SPLURT
Ready for the fight.
34TH ST
FORCEPS! I NEED FORCEPS...
HEY, UGLY. I'M BLAA-AACKK...
ZZZTTT
ZZZZTT
ZZZZZTTT
EISNER

chapter six

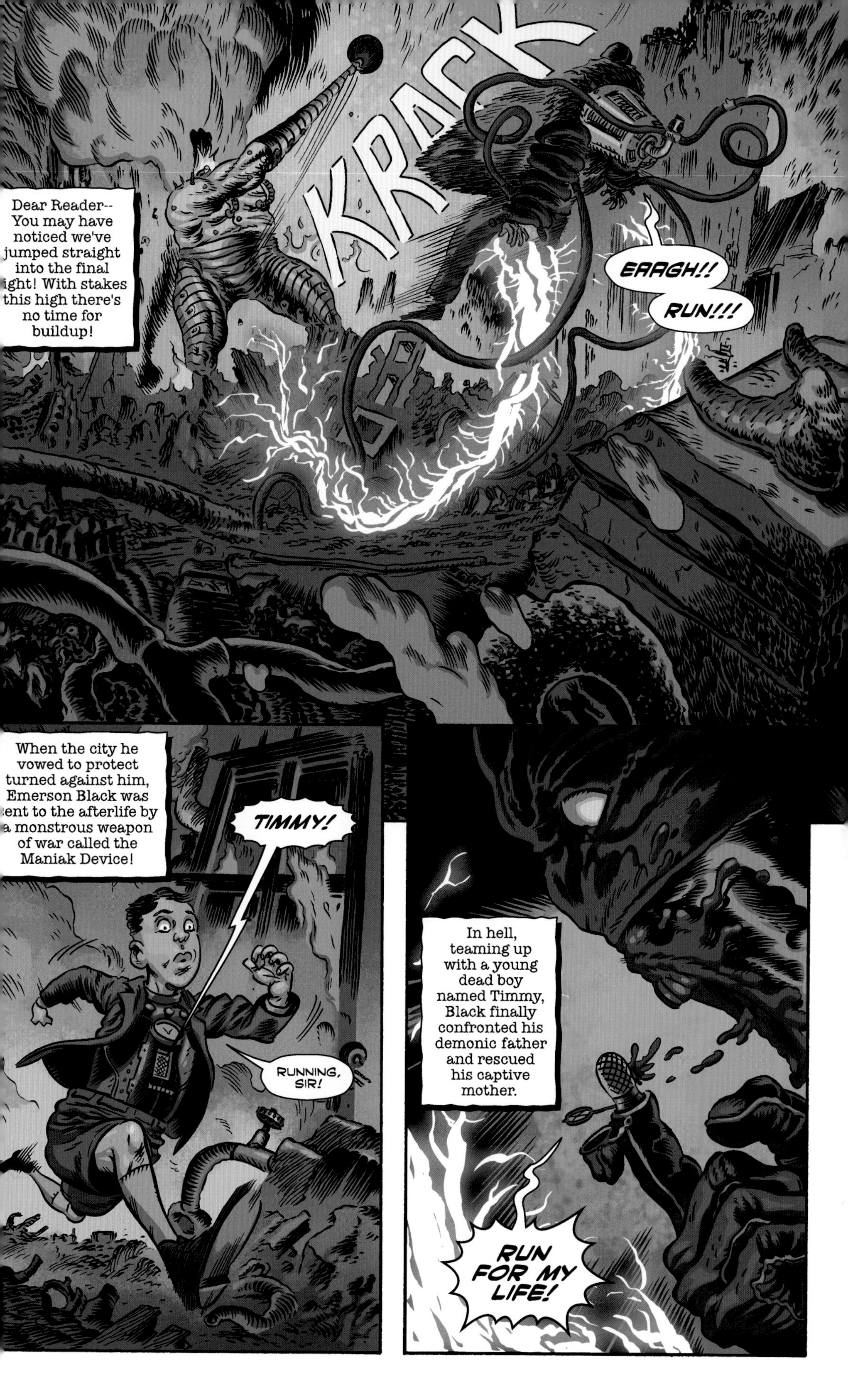
KRACK
Dear Reader-- You may have noticed we've jumped straight into the final ight! With stakes this high there's no time for buildup!
EAAGH!!
RUN!!!
When the city he vowed to protect turned against him, Emerson Black was ent to the afterlife by a monstrous weapon of war called the Maniak Device!
TIMMY!
RUNNING, SIR!
In hell, teaming up with a young dead boy named Timmy, Black finally confronted his demonic father and rescued his captive mother.
RUN FOR MY LIFE!

YOU KNOW WHERE TO GO, TIMMY!
Black's mother rebirthed Emerson and Timmy back into the land of the living to confront the Maniak, now turned against Coal City!
YOU KNOW WHAT TO DO!
Black may be back, but what's his new plan of attack?
KAPOW
THERE!
HOPE I'M NOT TOO LATE, MR. BLACK!
MR. BLACK?
RRGG...
ZZZZZRRRKK

Funny.
Always thought I held the power of Coal City in my bare hands.
OUCH
Turns out I was wrong.
I was wrong about EVERYTHING.

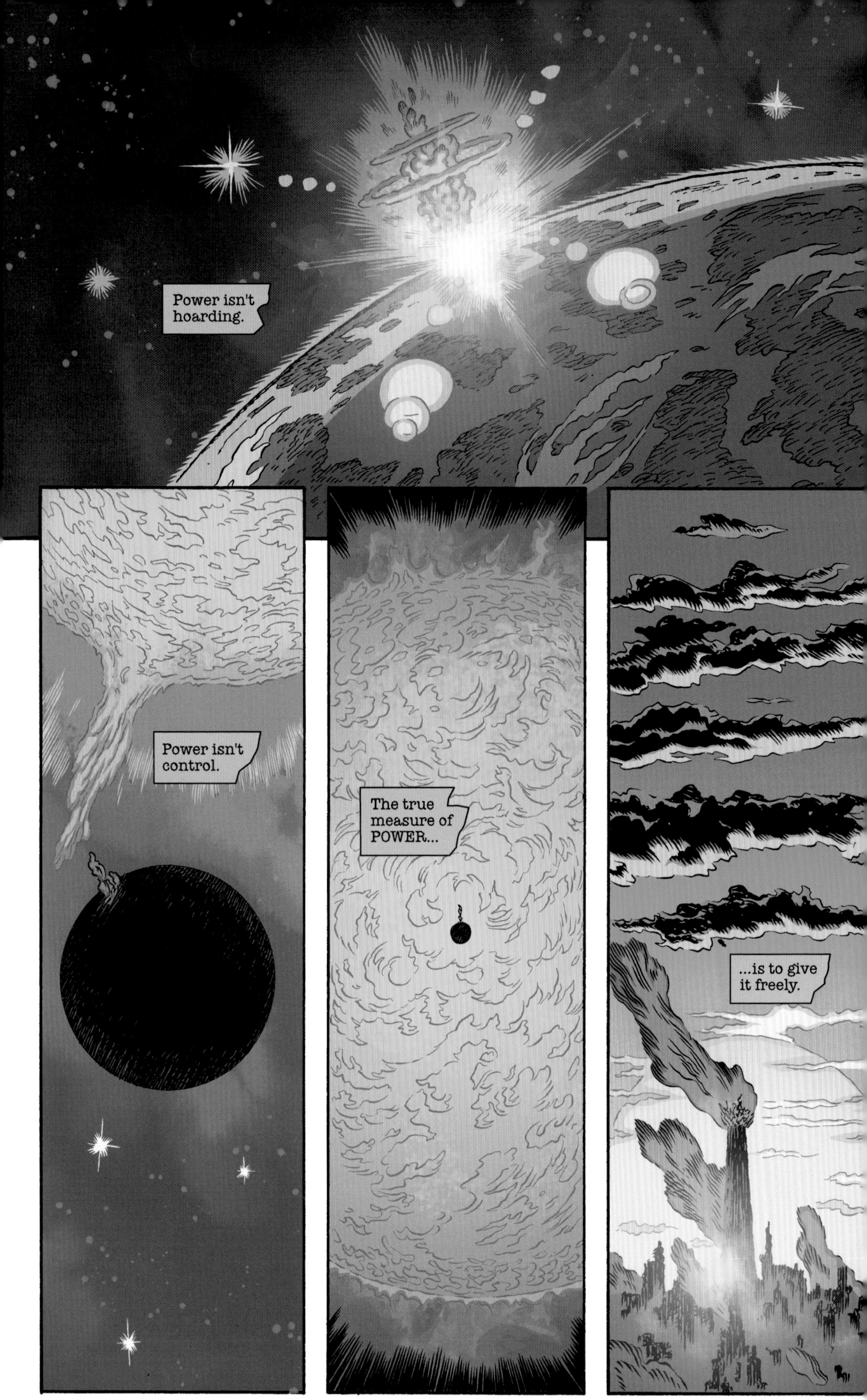

Power isn't hoarding.
Power isn't control.
The true measure of POWER...
...is to give it freely.

YOU DID IT, SIR. YOU SAVED THE CITY.
SIR?
ZZT
ZZT
ZZT

SINISTER
GET YER ARSES IN GEAR!
0101
350
MAYOR, BLACK POWER HAS BEEN SEIZED FROM THE BBA AND OWNERSHIP ASSIGNED DIRECTLY TO COAL CITY.
YOUR POINTS ARE AT A RECORD HIGH, MAYOR.
EXCELLENT.
MAYOR
JUST LIKE THE OLD PLAYGROUND DAYS, HEY, BEN?
SLOP

EXCELLENT? NO, IT'S HORRIBLE! ACTS OF GOD AND/OR BLACK ARE NOT COVERED UNDER ANY INSURANCE.
AND THE COSTS OF RESTORING COAL CITY, EVEN WITH THE PROJECTED REVENUE OF BLACK'S POWER PLANT, WILL BANKRUPT US.
FEELING PECKISH...
CALM DOWN, LUNDER. HAVE A SNACK.
WE DON'T NEED TO OWN THE HORSE, JUST PARADE HER UP AND DOWN THE STREET A LITTLE.
LET THE PEOPLE HOLD THE REINS JUST LONG ENOUGH TO LEAD HER TO MARKET.
OIL
KNOCK KNOCK
BE A DEAR AND GET THAT, WILL YOU?
?
OIL
BLUNDER, HAVE YOU MET THE YOUNG HEIR TO THE BLACK FORTUNE?
HE'S LOOKING TO INVEST.

HOW DID IT GO, MASTER TIMMY?
THE UPFRONT WAS ASTRONOMICAL, BUT ONCE WE TRIPLE THE POWER FEES IT WON'T BE LONG BEFORE WE'RE BACK IN THE...
...BLACK.
SLAM
THERE'S A WAR AGAINST THE MIDDLE CLASS. I NEED TO KNOW YOU ARE READY TO FIGHT.
THEY WON'T STAND A CHANCE, SIR.
THATTA BOY. SEND THEM BACK TO THEIR PUBLIC SCHOOLS AND STAGNANT WAGES.
IT'S A LOT OF RESPONSIBILITY TO LEAD A CITY.
AND WITH GREAT RESPONSIBILITY MUST COME GREAT...
POWER.
The End? Or the dark beginnings of the next insidious chapter of THE BLACK SINISTER?
Until the next time, Dark Believer. Just remember, always bet on Black!

My transition from movies back to comics wasn't without its speed bumps. Dark Horse was great in welcoming me back and hiring me to draw stories in *Eerie* and *Creepy*, and a *Lobster Johnson* one-shot. I enjoyed the hell out of all of the experiences, but I still felt a little wary of my renewed comic-booking as I kicked the tires on new creator-owned work. As bombastic as *The Black Sinister* is, it began on shaky legs. Think more ostrich chick and less fawn.

Everything I create starts with a sketch . . . well, lots of sketches. I draw constantly, and the root of *TBS* began as a simple doodle of a guy wearing a mask that's way too tight. As I refined him, a story began to percolate: What if the self-appointed savior of a city was actually its worst enemy? Basically, what if Batman was a real a-hole? The story I concocted was small and kind of subtle . . . and I didn't know what to do with it.

That's when the mighty Kaare Andrews swooped in and saved my bacon. As much as I appreciated what I had, I knew it needed more. With a strong desire to focus on getting my drawing chops back, I asked Kaare if he wanted to write it. Kaare is one of my best pals, and while we've dabbled with collaborations, we've never really cut loose on something big. I pitched him my one-line concept, sent him some art and the name, and he did what he does best: he fed it copious amounts of Pop Rocks, double espresso, and raw meat!

The story grew, and the zanier it became, the more excited I became. Suddenly we were writing and drawing with sticks of dynamite, and nothing could be crazy enough. We approached Brendan Wright with the idea, originally conceived as a two- or three-issue miniseries (my confidence to do something longer than that wasn't quite there yet), but it quickly became a serialized story in *Dark Horse Presents* instead. We loved the idea of cutting it into eight-page chunks and jamming as much as we always intended to do into forty-eight pages.

This is only a smattering of what I sketched up for the series. There's a few false starts, a very early version of the cover, and a whole lot of bonkers sketches. Everyone involved thanks you for picking up our slice of madness! Read it lots and lots!!!

—Troy Nixey

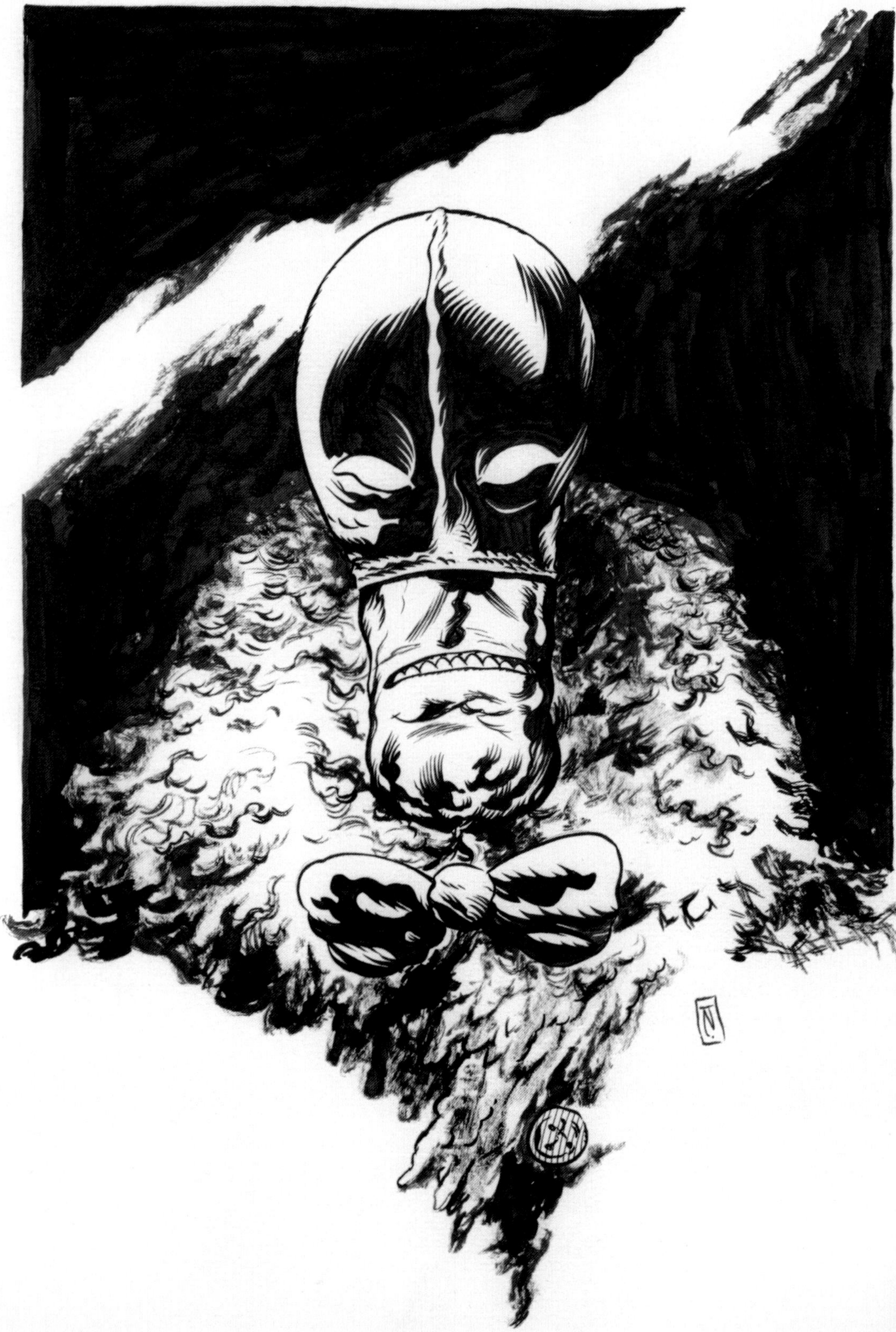

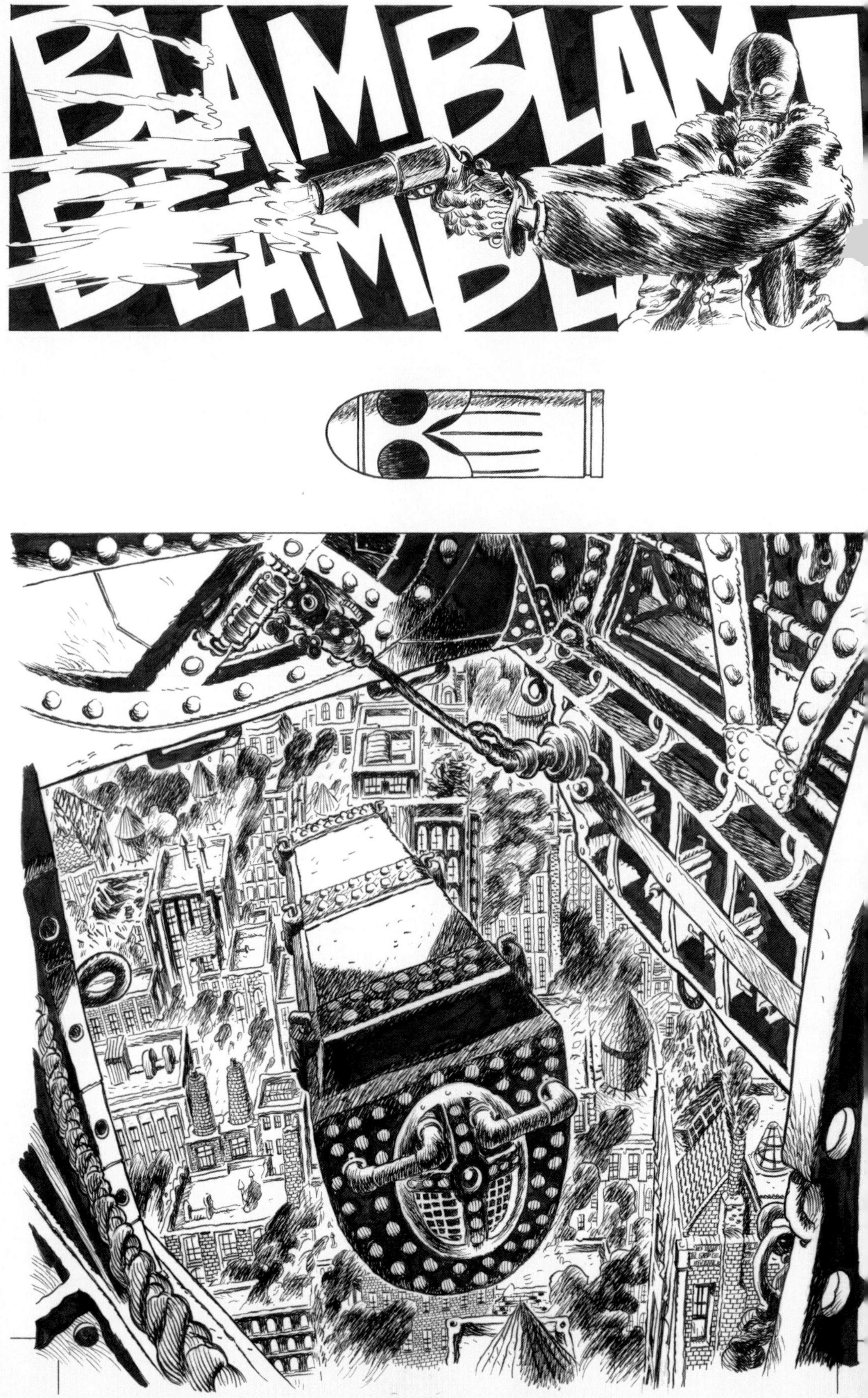
BLAMBLAM
BLAMBL

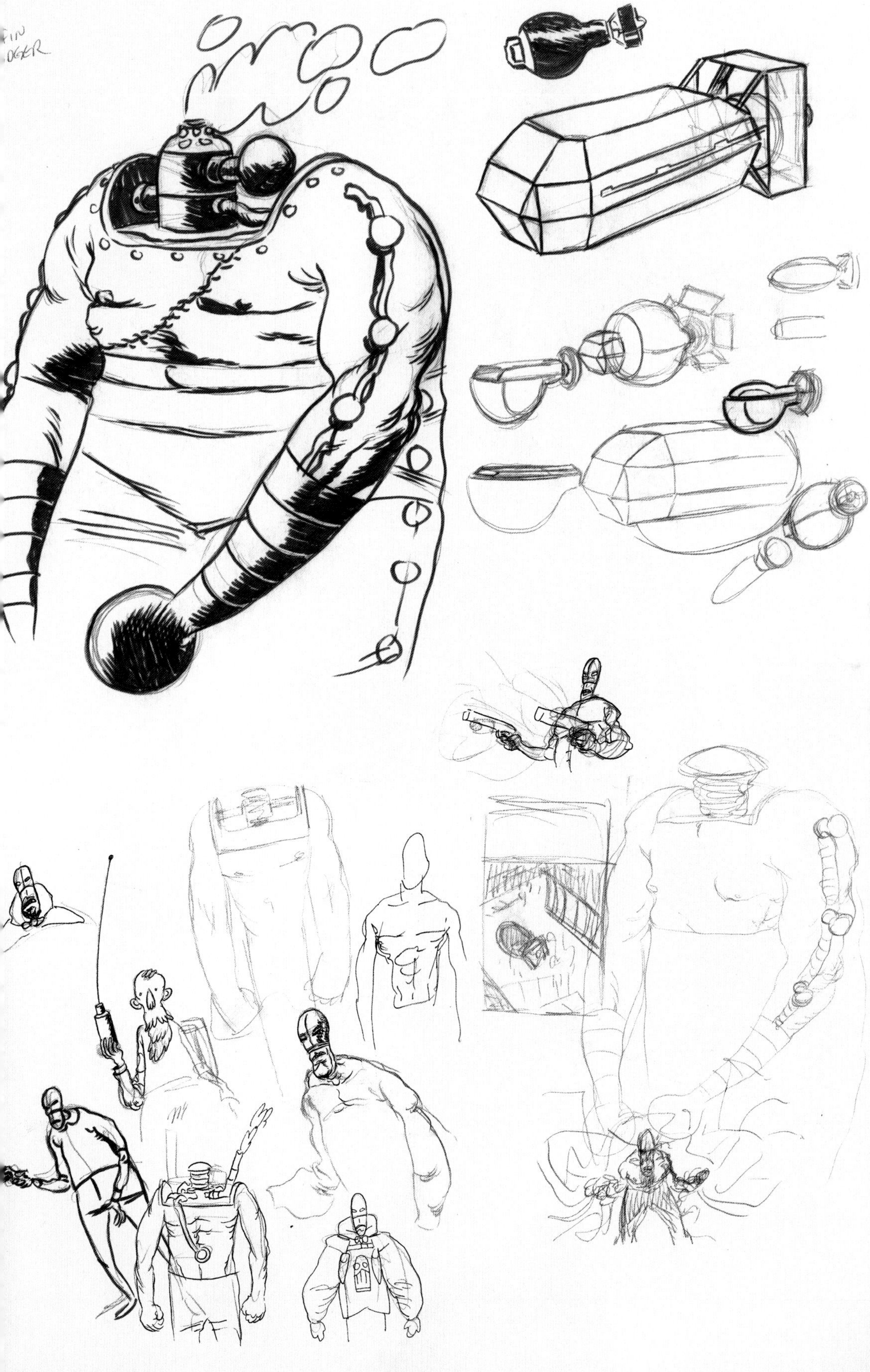

CALL THE COPS...
BLAM BLAM
CHAPTER ONE!
DEATH RIDES A BULLET...!
1

TBS-1.1

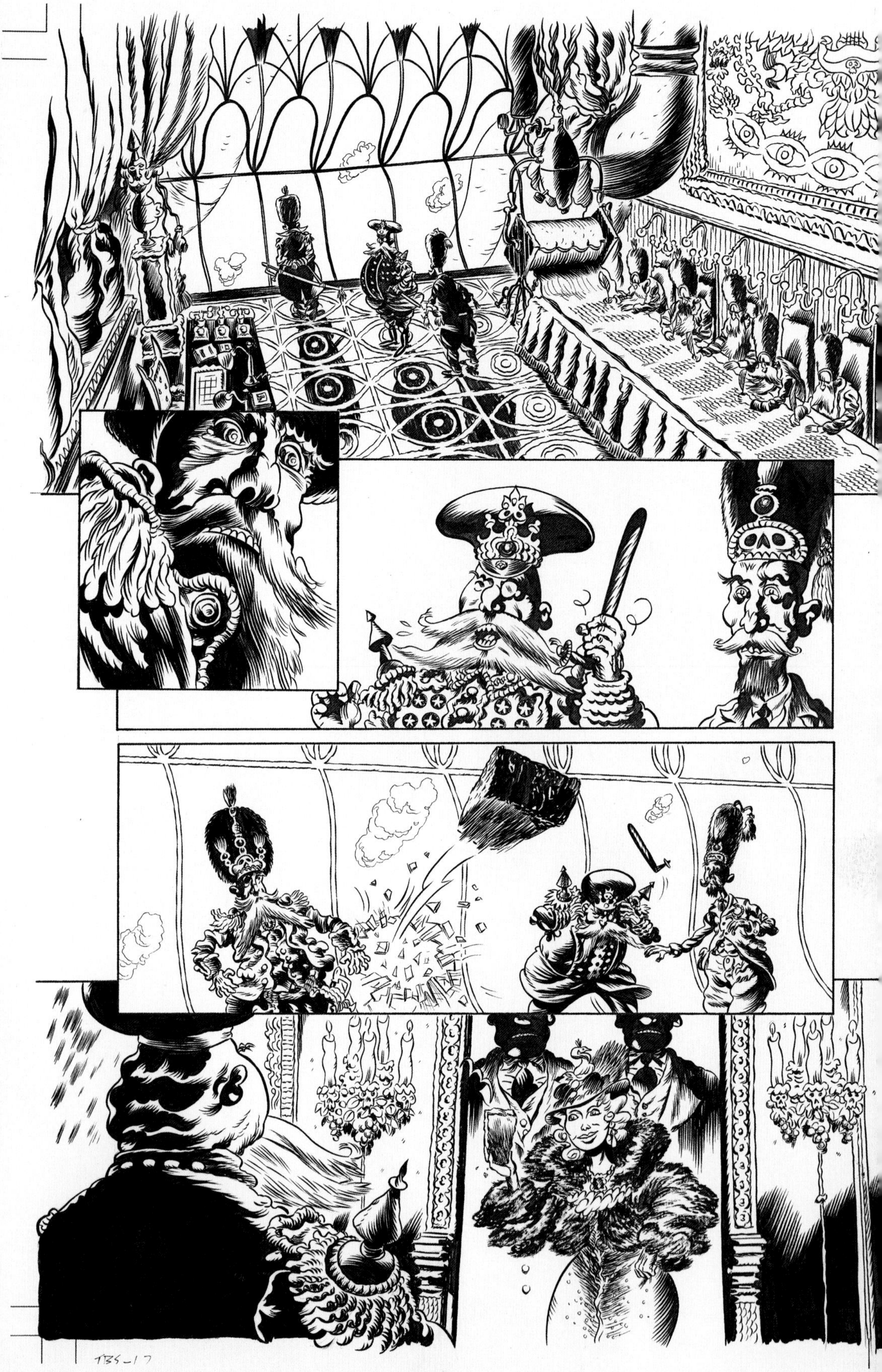

TBS-17